English Practice Year 2

Question Book

Emma Scott

Name _____

Schofield & Sims

Introduction

The **Schofield & Sims English Practice Year 2 Question Book** uses step-by-step practice to develop children's understanding of key English concepts. It covers every Year 2 objective in the 2014 National Curriculum programme of study.

The structure

This book is split into units, which are based on the key areas of the English curriculum for Year 2. These are:

- Grammar
- Punctuation
- Spelling
- Vocabulary
- Reading comprehension.

Each double-page spread follows a consistent 'Practise', 'Extend' and 'Apply' sequence designed to deepen and reinforce learning. Each objective also includes a 'Remember' box that reminds children of the key information needed to help answer the questions.

There are three reading comprehension units in this book. Each reading comprehension unit is linked by an overarching theme and includes a fiction, non-fiction and poetry text. Each text is accompanied by a set of comprehension questions, which practise reading skills such as inference, retrieval, summarising, prediction and analysis of word choice.

Additionally, a 'Writing skills' section allows children to apply the skills they have developed throughout the book in an extended writing task. The writing task is inspired by the themes covered in the reading comprehension texts and gives opportunities for children to showcase their creative writing.

At the back of the book, there is a 'Final practice' section. Here, mixed questions are used to check children's understanding of the knowledge and skills acquired throughout the book and identify any areas that need to be revisited.

A mastery approach

The **Primary Practice English** series follows a knowledge-based mastery approach. The books have a focus on learning with purpose to improve children's ability across all areas of English and to link learning in grammar, punctuation, spelling, vocabulary, reading and writing. There is frequent, varied practice and application of concepts to improve children's confidence when using their skills. A strong emphasis is given to vocabulary enrichment, reading for pleasure and reading stamina.

Assessment and checking progress

A 'Final practice' section is provided at the end of this book to check progress against the Year 2 English objectives. Children are given a target time of 45 minutes to complete this section, which is marked out of 25. Once complete, it enables them to assess their new knowledge and skills independently and to see the areas where they might need more practice.

Online answers

Answers for every question in this book are available to download from the **Schofield & Sims** website. The answers are accompanied by detailed explanations where helpful. There is also a progress chart, allowing children to track their learning as they complete each set of questions, and an editable certificate.

Contents

Nouns and noun phrases

Remember

Nouns are words that name people, places and things. Common nouns name everyday things. For example: 'pencil', 'chair', 'balloon'. Proper nouns name people, places, months and days of the week. They must start with a capital letter. For example: 'Jacob', 'London', 'November', 'Wednesday'.

A noun phrase is a noun and the words that go with it. 'The pencil', 'that chair' and 'some balloons' are all simple noun phrases.

Practise

1. Sort these nouns into the table.

| Manchester | pasta | coins | Jack | balloon |
| pony | August | France | plate | Tuesday |

Proper nouns	Common nouns

2. Tick to show which type of noun is used in each sentence.

Sentence	Proper noun	Common noun
a. I bought some new cushions.		
b. On Sunday, I went cycling.		
c. Grandad loves reading.		
d. The baby cried.		

3 Circle the nouns and noun phrases in the cloud.

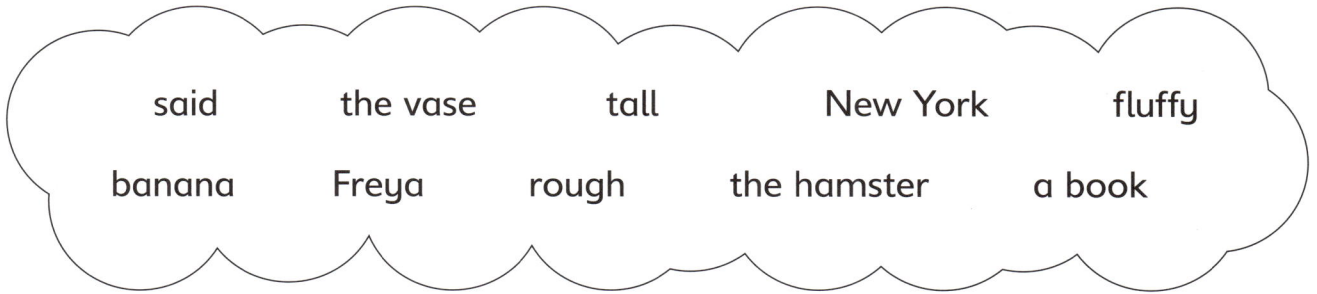

said   the vase   tall   New York   fluffy

banana   Freya   rough   the hamster   a book

4 Complete these sentences using the nouns and noun phrases in **Question 3**.

a. I pack a _____ every day for my snack.

b. _____ placed the flowers in _____.

c. _____ is a very busy city full of skyscrapers.

d. I am going to buy _____ by my favourite author.

e. At night, I can hear _____ in its cage.

Apply

5 a. Write the names of **three** people. They might be your family, your friends or famous people.

_____   _____   _____

b. Write the names of **three** places in the world. They might be countries or landmarks that you have visited or would like to visit.

_____   _____   _____

c. Write a sentence a the name and a place from **Questions 5a** and **5b**.

_____

_____

Adjectives

Remember

An adjective is a word that describes a noun. For example: 'the **tall** giraffe', 'my **wavy** hair', 'a **juicy** orange'.

Practise

1 Circle the best adjective to describe each picture.

a.

excited   tasty   muddy

b.

brave   quick   bright

c.

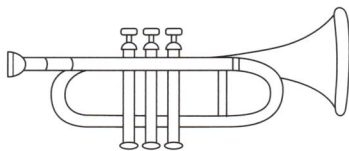

noisy   clumsy   quick

d.

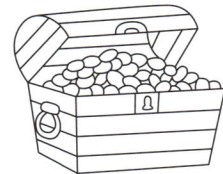

ancient   sweet   annoying

e.

calm   soft   angry

f.

new   crazy   juicy

2 Tick to show the adjectives that describe the ball.

square ☐   round ☐   pink ☐   black ☐

smelly ☐   white ☐   happy ☐   smooth ☐

〉〉 Extend

3 Underline the adjectives in these sentences. There may be more than one.

    a.   The graceful butterfly flew into my garden.

    b.   The cool breeze and the calm sea relaxed me.

    c.   The modern house was built in the new city.

    d.   The elegant lady wore a purple and gold hat.

4 Complete these sentences using the adjectives in the box. Use each word once.

> angry   bright   adorable   squeaky   kind

    a.   The sun was so _____ that I needed to wear my sunglasses.

    b.   My new kitten is _____.

    c.   My teacher was very _____ and helped me with my work.

    d.   The floorboards in my house are really _____.

    e.   Jo was _____ when the slugs ate her cabbages.

☁ Apply

5 Write **two** adjectives to describe each picture.

    a.

    _____

    _____

    b.

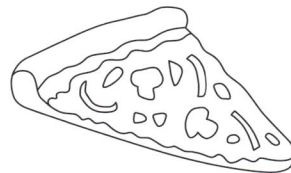

    _____

    _____

6 Write **one** sentence about **one** picture in **Question 5**. Use **two** adjectives.

_____

Expanded noun phrases

Remember

Adjectives can be added to noun phrases to describe the noun in more detail. For example: 'the kitten' becomes 'the **tiny** kitten'. More than one adjective can be used to expand the noun phrase. For example: 'the **tiny, fluffy** kitten'.

Practise

1. Circle the adjectives and underline the nouns in the expanded noun phrases.

   a. a sparkly gem

   b. the deep lake

   c. a haunted mansion

   d. some cold ice cream

   e. a brave knight

   f. the talented singer

2. **a.** Tick the **six** expanded noun phrases.

running quickly	☐	some salty crisps	☐
the crazy frogs	☐	far away	☐
playing a game	☐	a friendly neighbour	☐
the soft sand	☐	a wobbly jelly	☐
ring bells	☐	the green grass	☐

   b. Write the **six** nouns from the expanded noun phrases.

   ______________________ ______________________

   ______________________ ______________________

   ______________________ ______________________

3 Write expanded noun phrases about the pictures. Use **one** adjective from the box in each phrase.

delicious	strong	long	ugly	sad	woolly

a.

the _____ woman

b.

a _____ sheep

c.

some _____ cakes

d.

the _____ man

e.

an _____ troll

f.

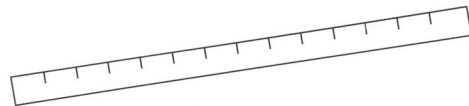

his _____ ruler

Apply

4 Write **two** expanded noun phrases using these adjectives. Use at least **one** adjective from the box. One has been done for you.

black	fluffy	young	furry	ugly	~~slimy~~	~~smelly~~	dark

a. <u>some slimy, smelly frogs</u>

b. _____

Present and past tenses

Remember

The present tense describes something happening now. For example: '**I walk** to school'. The past tense describes something that has already happened. For example: '**I walked** to school'.

Use the present or past tense with –ing to show that an action is continuing. For example: '**I am walking** to school' or '**I was walking** to school'.

Practise

1 Tick the sentences that are in the present tense and cross the sentences that are in the past tense.

The birds were singing in the trees. ☐

The postman delivers the letters. ☐

The secretary was typing the letter. ☐

Worms live under the soil. ☐

Karim is having a rest. ☐

Emily made a daisy chain. ☐

Extend

2 Choose a verb from the box and write it in the correct tense to complete each sentence. One has been done for you.

fly   ~~smell~~   slither   fry

a. My grandad was ___smelling___ the flowers in his garden.

b. The geese were _____ south for the winter.

c. My aunty was _____ an egg.

d. The snake was _____ around hunting for prey.

③ Write **one** sentence in the present tense about what is happening in each picture.

a.  _____

_____

b.  _____

_____

Tip Remember that the present tense is used to describe something that is happening now.

🗨 Apply

④ Write **one** sentence about what you were doing yesterday at the time shown on each clock.

a. 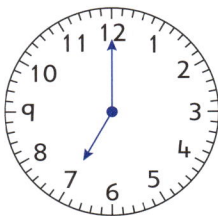 _____

_____

morning

b.  _____

_____

noon

c. 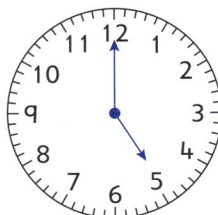 _____

_____

afternoon

Verbs

Remember

Verbs are 'doing' words. They change depending on who is doing the action. For example: 'I **wave** goodbye' or 'He **waves** goodbye'. Verbs are also 'being' words. For example: 'I **am** a teacher' or 'She **is** clever'.

Practise

1. Draw lines to match each picture to the correct verb.

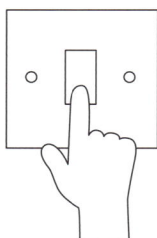

| pull | smile | switch | sing | fetch |

2. Sort these verbs into the table.

jump   wave   is   play   am   was
shout   has   see   whisper   do   eat

Doing words	Being words

▶ Extend

3 Underline all the verbs in these sentences.

a. I tiptoed up the stairs quietly.

b. Jon screamed at the giant spider.

c. Finally, I completed my homework.

d. She has a pet fish, a dog and a lizard.

e. We shut the gate in the farmer's field.

f. I am ready for the match.

4 Complete the sentences using the verbs in the box.

is am play pushed plays crouched

a. The radio _____ loud music.

b. I _____ down to look under the bed.

c. Hamza _____ me on the swing.

d. I _____ the tallest in my class.

e. We _____ tennis every weekend.

f. Rebecca _____ my best friend.

☁ Apply

5 Write **three** sentences about what you did at the weekend. One has been done for you.

a. I played football.

b. _____

c. _____

Adverbs

Adverbs provide more information more about an action (a verb). They often end in –ly. For example: 'George whispered **quietly**'. An adverb can also explain where, when or how often something happens. For example: 'Sophia waits **outside**' or 'I will see you **soon**'.

Practise

1 Circle the adverbs in these sentences.

   a. The children splashed playfully in the sea.

   b. The sun shone brightly in the sky.

   c. Cautiously, Ava creeps down the stairs.

   d. The monkey grabbed the banana cheekily.

   e. I often go to the shop.

2 Sort these adverbs into the table.

> happily   quickly   inside   slowly
> later   outside   yesterday   angrily

How the action is done	Where the action is done	When the action is done

3 Draw lines to match each adverb to one with the opposite meaning. One has been done for you.

joyfully	quickly
angrily	sadly
slowly	calmly
boldly	successfully
unsuccessfully	shyly

4 Underline the correct adverb to complete each sentence.

a. Shobna skipped **loudly / soon / happily** to the theme park.

b. The choir sang **usually / beautifully / angrily** at the concert.

c. Freddie licked the lolly **almost / greedily / successfully**.

d. **Quietly / Almost / Sometimes** my mum takes us to the cinema.

Apply

5 Rewrite these sentences with an adverb to make them more interesting.

a. Lily ran to catch the bus.

_____

b. The puppy chewed the slipper.

_____

c. We waited.

_____

Sentence types

Practise

(1) Tick to show whether each sentence is a statement, question or command.

Sentence	Statement	Question	Command
a. My brother is older than me.			
b. What are we having for dinner tonight?			
c. Carry that box to the car.			

(2) Write the sentence type.

a. What a lovely surprise this is! _____

b. What time will you be there? _____

c. Fetch that stick. _____

Extend

(3) Write a statement to answer each question.

a. What is the girl holding?

_____

b. What is the boy building?

_____

4 Write a question to correspond with the pictures and statements.

a.

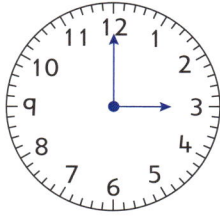

_____

It is 3 o'clock.

b.

_____

A knight is riding the horse.

5 Tim needs some help tidying the house. Write **four** commands using the verbs in the box. One has been done for you.

| mop | dust | ~~put~~ | vacuum | clean | polish | sweep | fold |

a. Put the clothes in the washing machine. _____

b. _____

c. _____

d. _____

💭 **Apply**

6 Write **one** sentence of each type about this picture.

a. **Question:**

_____

b. **Exclamation:**

_____

Tip Remember that exclamation sentences begin with 'what' or 'how'.

Joining words

Joining words ('and', 'or', 'but', 'when', 'if', 'that' and 'because') give more information about the main idea in a sentence and link ideas together.

Co-ordination words ('and', 'or', 'but') link separate ideas together. For example: 'I want pasta **but** Isla wants chips'. Subordination words ('when', 'if', 'that', 'because') join two clauses. For example: 'Theo saw flowers **when** he went outside'.

Practise

1 Circle the joining words in these sentences.

a. You can have a yoghurt or you can have fruit for dessert.

b. I went to the doctor because I was feeling ill.

c. It was raining but I still went for a walk.

d. I like chocolate cake and Tom likes carrot cake.

e. Greta was overjoyed when she won the competition.

f. Lewis enjoyed listening to the song that his brother sang.

2 Rewrite these sentences using 'if' or 'but' as joining words.

a. I like fish. I don't like chips.

_____

b. I promise to share the prize. I win the game.

_____

c. I want to swim. The water is warm.

_____

d. I fell over. It did not hurt.

_____

» Extend

3 Draw lines to match the beginnings and endings of these sentences.

Garden birds need more food when	it was my birthday.
My puppy gets a treat if	her mum gave her.
Suki rode the new bicycle that	it is winter.
I opened my presents because	he lifts his paw.

4 Choose the correct joining word from the box to complete these sentences.

> or   but

a. I like strawberries _____ I don't like cherries.

b. We could bake a cake _____ cookies.

c. Mohammed loves rugby _____ he hates tennis.

d. My class planted some seeds _____ some of the plants did not grow.

Apply

5 Complete these sentences using the joining words 'when', 'if', 'that' or 'because' and your own ideas.

a. The children played indoors _____.

b. The police officer chased the dog _____.

c. We can watch the film _____.

d. Lucy cheered _____.

Standard English

Remember

When writing and speaking, it is best to use Standard English. Standard English follows rules such as using the correct verb form in the sentence and choosing the correct words. For example: 'They done good' is non-Standard English. 'They did well' is Standard English.

Practise

1. Tick to show whether each sentence in the table is in Standard English or non-Standard English.

Sentence	Standard English	Non-Standard English
a. I done my homework yesterday.		
b. We was there.		
c. They went to the park.		
d. Dad won't give me no more snacks.		
e. She gave me a drink.		
f. I drew a picture.		

2. Draw lines to match the non-Standard English and Standard English versions of each sentence.

I gone for a walk.	You should have worn a coat.
They ain't got nothing new.	It was closed.
You should of worn a coat.	They haven't got anything new.
It were closed.	I went for a walk.

⟫ Extend

3 Circle the correct verb to complete these sentences in Standard English.

a. I **done / did** my homework yesterday.

b. He **ran / runned** the race in record time.

c. Mrs Murray **writ / wrote** the question on the board.

d. Grandma **ain't / hasn't** got many toys at her house.

e. The tyres **was / were** flat so we had to walk home.

4 Rewrite the underlined words so that these sentences are in Standard English.

a. You ran that race very <u>good</u>. _____

b. Tristan didn't see <u>nothing</u>. _____

c. It <u>were</u> closed. _____

d. Give me one of <u>them</u> crisps please. _____

Apply

5 Rewrite each sentence using Standard English.

a. It weren't me.

_____

b. Meera done good.

_____

c. Miss Ridge won't give me no pencil.

_____

d. I writ a great poem.

_____

Commas in lists

Remember

Commas can be used to separate items in a list. For example: 'I ordered a burger, fries, salad and a strawberry milkshake'. Do not use a comma before the word 'and' or before the last item in a list.

Practise

(1) Copy the comma below.

(2) Write commas in the correct places in these sentences.

a. I bought a pint of milk a loaf of bread and a chocolate cake.

b. The chocolate cake was covered with icing sprinkles and cherries.

c. My favourite book is all about aliens planets stars and comets.

d. I enjoy reading playing football exploring and swimming in the sea.

≫ Extend

(3) Rewrite these sentences using commas to replace 'and' where needed.

a. The Nile and the Amazon and the Rhine are rivers.

_____

b. Beagles and poodles and collies are breeds of dog.

_____

c. The fruit bowl contains pears and apples and plums and peaches.

_____

d. I have a pen and a rubber and a pencil and a ruler.

_____

4 Complete the sentences using these shopping lists.

a.

Pet shop
hay
sawdust
rabbit food
treats

b.

Newsagents
comic
sweets
stamps
newspaper

a. Abi went to the pet shop to buy _____

_____

b. Suresh went to the newsagents to buy _____

_____

Tip Remember that you need to use commas to separate the items in a list when the list is part of a sentence. Think carefully about where the commas should go.

Apply

5 a. Write **four** items on your own shopping list.

_____

_____

_____

_____

b. Turn your list into a sentence about what you need to buy. Include the correct punctuation.

_____

_____

Using different punctuation

Practise

1 Write the punctuation mark that each sentence describes.

   a. I am used at the end of a sentence to show that it is complete.   ——

   b. I am used at the end of a sentence that asks a question.   ——

   c. I am used at the end of a sentence to show strong feelings.   ——

2 Circle the correct punctuation to finish each sentence.

   a. Do you think it will snow today   ?   !   .

   b. We are going to the park   ?   !   .

   c. How lovely it is to see you all again   ?   !   .

   d. Today is a school day   ?   !   .

⟫ Extend

3 Write the words and the punctuation marks in the correct order so each sentence makes sense.

   a. favourite   pizza   food   My   .   is

   _____

   b. time   ?   the   What   train   leave   does

   _____

   c. adventure   What   !   exciting   had   we've   an   today

   _____

4 Rewrite these sentences using the correct punctuation.

a. saturday is my favourite day of the week

_____

b. what a brilliant teacher Mrs Jarvis is

_____

c. what shall we watch on the television tonight

_____

Apply

5 Add the missing punctuation to this postcard.

Dear Max

I am having the best time How
sunny and hot it is here What is the
weather like at home Today, I went
to the beach We packed a picnic with
sandwiches crisps cake and orange juice
I built a huge sandcastle decorated it
with shells and put a flag on top Then
I went for a paddle in the sea It was
so cold Mum bought me an ice cream
but a naughty seagull swooped down
and stole it right out of my hand
What have you been up to

See you soon

Sunita

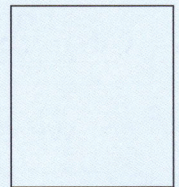

Tip Remember all the different types of punctuation you could add. There are
capital letters, commas, full stops, question marks and exclamation marks.

Apostrophes in shortened forms

Remember

Sometimes two words are pushed together to make a shorter word or contraction. An apostrophe is used to replace any letters that have been removed. For example: 'I am' becomes 'I'm'. Sometimes the shortened word is different from the original words. For example: 'will not' becomes 'won't'.

Practise

1 Draw lines to match the words to their shortened forms. One has been done for you.

is not	we're
I am	don't
we are	she's
they have	I'm
do not	isn't
she is	they've

2 a. Circle the shortened forms in this text.

> We've got a new puppy. We shouldn't let her run off. We're going to keep a close eye on her and make sure she's not chasing any squirrels! I'm sure she will behave herself. If she doesn't, then we're going to need to keep her on her lead for a little bit longer.

b. Choose **two** shortened forms and write them in full.

_____   _____

Extend

3 Write the shortened forms of these words using apostrophes.

a. have not _____

b. you are _____

c. we will _____

d. did not _____

e. can not _____

f. we have _____

4 Circle the shortened form in each sentence and write it as **two** words.

a. I don't like beans on toast. _____

b. He's my best friend. _____

c. My dad doesn't want a pet. _____

d. Where's the best place to go for a walk? _____

e. That's my favourite pair of boots! _____

f. We'll have to see if it rains tomorrow. _____

Apply

5 Write **four** sentences of your own using shortened forms.

a. _____

_____

b. _____

_____

c. _____

_____

d. _____

_____

Apostrophes for possession

✏️ Practise

(1) Circle the words that have an apostrophe for possession.

> Eliza's coat was hanging on the peg yesterday, but today Charles's hat is hanging there. Amari's bag is on the floor and Alexandra's bag is on the bench. The teacher's laptop is on her desk. Michael's books are in his tray.

» Extend

(2) Use an apostrophe and an 's' to describe each picture.

a. Erin

_____

b. Omar

_____

c. Jill

_____

d. Kofi

_____

3 Rewrite these sentences using an apostrophe to show that something belongs to something.

a. The sofa has cushions.

_____

b. The book has pages.

_____

c. The dinosaur has claws.

_____

Apply

4 Write **one** sentence to describe each picture. Use an apostrophe to show possession in each sentence.

a.

George

_____
_____

b.

Shireen

_____
_____

5 Draw a picture of your own and write **one** sentence to describe what is happening. Use an apostrophe to show possession.

_____
_____

The /ur/, /or/, /s/ and /u/ sounds

Remember

Some sounds have alternative ways of spelling them. The /ur/ sound can be spelt 'or' after 'w'. For example: w**or**m. The /or/ sound can be spelt 'ar' after 'w'. For example: w**ar**m. The /s/ sound can be spelt 'c' before 'e', 'i' and 'y'. For example: pen**c**il. The /u/ sound can be spelt 'o'. For example: d**o**zen.

Practise

1 Sort these words into the table depending on which sound they have after the 'w'.

> worm   word   warm   towards
> world   work   worth   war

/ur/ sound	/or/ sound

2 Circle the words with the /u/ sound spelt 'o'.

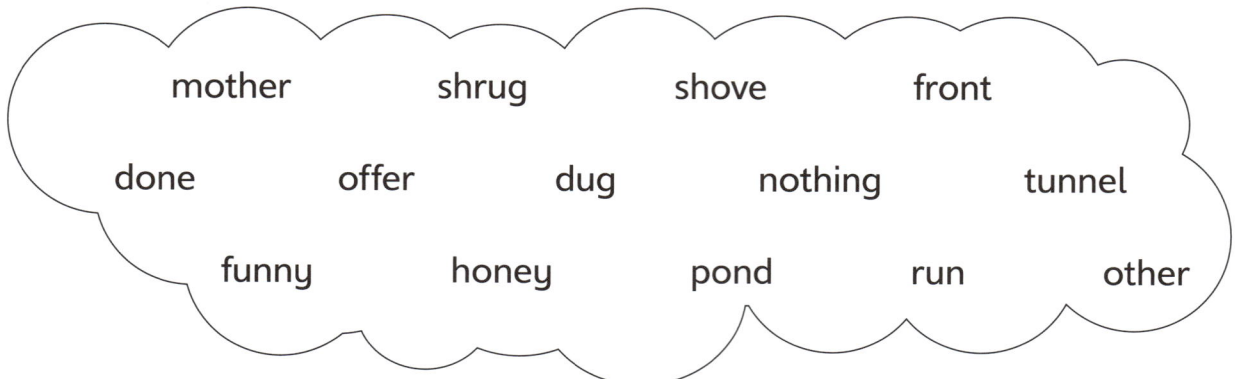

mother   shrug   shove   front
done   offer   dug   nothing   tunnel
funny   honey   pond   run   other

3) Complete these sentences using the words from the box.

towards	dice	word	warm	choice

a. Inside the cabin, it was _____ and cosy.

b. We need _____ to play the game.

c. If I had the _____ I would like to walk to school.

d. Randall quickly ran _____ me.

e. We used a dictionary to find the correct spelling of the

_____ .

4) Write the correct words with an /u/ sound under the pictures.

a.

b.

c.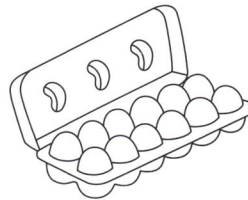

d.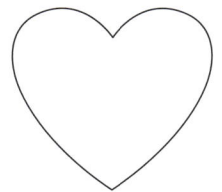

_____   _____   _____   _____

Apply

5) Write **two** sentences of your own. Use at least **one** word from the box in each sentence.

discover	honey	nothing	oven	son	brother	month	above

a. _____

_____

b. _____

_____

Words beginning 'kn', 'gn' and 'wr'

Remember

Sometimes words beginning with the /n/ sound are spelt with 'kn' or 'gn' instead of 'n'. For example: '**kn**ight' and '**gn**ome'.

The /r/ sound can be spelt with 'wr' rather than 'r' at the beginning of words. For example: '**wr**ite'.

Practise

1 Tick the things where the /n/ sound is spelt with 'kn'.

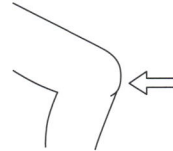

☐   ☐   ☐   ☐   ☐

2 Write the letters for the missing sound in each word by choosing the correct letters from the box.

gn   kn   wr

a. _____ome

b. _____ite

c. _____ow

d. _____en

e. _____at

f. _____ot

g. _____ock

h. _____u

Tip Try each pair of letters from the box before the letters in the question to see if they make a word. If you're not sure, use a dictionary to check if the word exists.

3 Complete these sentences using the 'kn' or 'gn' words from the box.

> knead   gnome   knows   knit   gnaw

a. I am going to _____ a jumper.

b. Clara has a _____ in her garden.

c. Once the dough is ready, you can _____ it.

d. My pet rabbit likes to _____ on a carrot.

e. Marvin _____ the way.

4 Write the correct spelling of each word on the line.

a.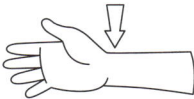

_____

b.

_____

c.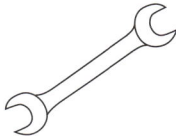

_____

d.

_____

Apply

5 Complete this crossword using the clues.

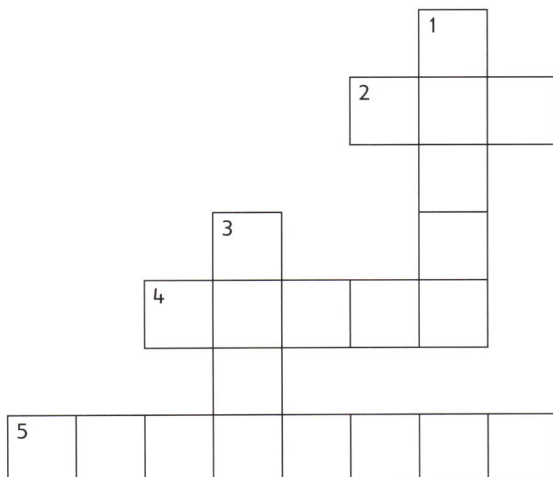

Across

2. An African animal.

4. You use this to cut food.

5. A craft using wool.

Down

1. A garden ornament.

3. A small insect.

Words ending 'le', 'el' and 'ey'

Remember

Sounds at the end of words can be spelt in different ways. The /l/ sound is spelt 'le' after most consonants. For example: 'tab**le**'. The /l/ sound is spelt 'el' after 'm', 'n', 'r', 's', 'v' or 'w'. For example: 'jew**el**'. There are some exceptions. For example: 'chap**el**'. The /ee/ sound is sometimes spelt 'ey'. For example: 'monk**ey**'. These spellings usually appear at the end of a two-syllable word.

Practise

1 Sort these words into the table.

> table   jewel   chapel   apple   prickle
>
> kettle   tunnel   squirrel   single   camel

'le'	'el'

2 Write the words from the box under the correct picture.

> jockey   honey   turkey   key   trolley   chimney

a.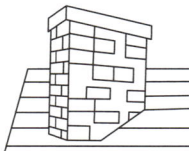

_____

b.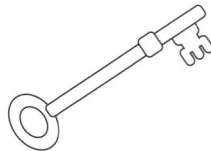

_____

c.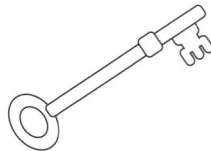

_____

d.

_____

e.

_____

f.

_____

» Extend

3 Write the correct letters 'le' or 'el' to complete each word.

a. beet_____   b. wobb_____   c. lev_____

d. ridd_____   e. funn_____   f. mod_____

4 Underline the words in the letter that are spelt incorrectly. Write the correct spellings for each word on the lines.

> Welcome to our holiday home!
>
> You can use the kettel to make a cup of tea. There are some appels in the fruit bowl and a homemade trifel in the fridge. You can find clean towles in the bathroom.
>
> You may wish to visit the pebbel beach or the beautiful chaple in town.
>
> Have a lovely stay.

_____   _____   _____

_____   _____   _____

Apply

5 Find all **five** words with the ending 'ey' in the word search.

F	G	H	O	C	K	E	Y	P	K
A	V	N	U	Y	A	J	U	U	M
Z	B	I	Z	D	A	R	H	L	T
C	Q	O	S	T	W	T	P	L	X
T	K	I	D	N	E	Y	R	E	M
C	H	U	T	N	E	Y	O	Y	P
P	P	U	Z	C	N	G	H	U	P
K	D	R	J	O	U	R	N	E	Y
E	U	B	B	N	N	Z	V	D	I
P	S	G	I	Q	Y	O	L	H	J

pulley   journey   hockey

chutney   kidney

Tip Look at the word search carefully because the words can run horizontally or vertically.

Adding the suffix –es

Remember

To make the plural of most words, add –s at the end of the word. For example: 'dog' becomes 'dog**s**'. Words that end in 'y' and have a vowel before the 'y' follow this rule. For example: 'toy' becomes 'toy**s**'.

However, if a word ends in 'y' and has a consonant before the 'y', then the 'y' is changed to an 'i' **before** –es is added. For example: 'berr**y**' becomes 'berr**ies**'.

Practise

1 Sort these words into the table.

| baby | key | lorry | party | valley | toy | city | enemy |

Words with a consonant before 'y'	Words with a vowel before 'y'

2 Complete the sentences using the words in the box.

| babies | lorries | cities | enemies |

a. The _____ got stuck in a traffic jam.

b. London, Manchester and Newcastle are all _____ in England.

c. The opponents in the football match were _____ .

d. In the nursery, the _____ played happily all day.

➤➤ Extend

3 Write the plural form of these words.

a. lady _____

b. story _____

c. puppy _____

d. cherry _____

e. butterfly _____

f. memory _____

4 Write the plural of the word in brackets in these sentences.

a. The _____ (pony) were grazing in the field.

b. The _____ (boy) ran down the street.

c. I went to lots of _____ (party) last summer.

d. Quietly, the _____ (spy) watched the house.

e. A continent is a group of _____ (country).

f. Mum carried _____ (tray) of plants from the garden centre.

Tip Check if the noun ends in a 'y'. If it does, check if it has a consonant before it. If the noun has a consonant before the 'y', the 'y' will need to change to an 'i' before the suffix is added.

☁ Apply

5 This is Borg. He comes from the planet Zorg. Explain to him how you would change the word 'fairy' from singular to plural.

_____

_____

Words ending 'tion', 'ge' and 'dge'

Remember

Some words end with similar sounds but have different spellings. The /sh/ sound is spelt 'ti' in words ending in 'tion'. For example: 'sta**ti**on'. The /j/ sound is spelt 'ge' at the end of a word if it comes after a consonant or a long vowel sound (when the vowel sound is stretched out). For example: 'ca**ge**'. The /j/ sound is spelt 'dge' at the end of a word if it comes immediately after a short vowel. For example: 'he**dge**'.

Practise

1 Write the missing letters to complete these words.

a. posi_____   **b.** educa_____   **c.** direc_____

2 Circle the letter that comes before the /j/ sound in each of these words. Tick to show whether it is a long vowel sound or a short vowel sound. One has been done for you.

Word	Long vowel sound	Short vowel sound
a. p a g (e)	✓	
b. s t a g e		
c. f u d g e		
d. s m u d g e		

Extend

3 Read the clues and write the missing letters to complete the 'tion' words. The first letter has been given to help you.

a. a place where you catch a train   s_____

b. to ask something   q_____

c. a part of a whole   f_____

d. something you go to hospital for   o_____

4. Write the missing word endings 'ge' or 'dge' to complete these sentences.

   a. As soon as we saw snow, we headed for the hills with our sle_____.

   b. Did you know that a troll lives under that bri_____?

   c. The man was red in the face with ra_____.

   d. The tiger prowled around his ca_____ staring at the visitors.

   e. The fri_____ kept the milk cold.

   f. There was a small villa_____ at the e_____ of the large town.

Apply

5. **a.** Find all **five** words with the ending 'tion' in the word search.

P	J	T	W	D	I	B	A	I	S
T	C	C	A	U	T	I	O	N	Z
R	O	V	G	P	X	F	M	C	P
Z	P	W	A	O	P	T	I	O	N
M	N	B	C	M	R	C	M	S	Q
O	D	G	T	B	S	U	J	G	Z
T	L	H	I	Y	L	F	I	C	Q
I	E	Y	O	A	K	B	G	Y	O
O	H	S	N	E	Y	L	K	K	O
N	S	E	C	T	I	O	N	Y	T

action   caution   motion

option   section

Tip Look at the word search carefully because the words can run horizontally or vertically.

   b. Write **one** sentence using **one** word from the word search.

   _____

6. Write **two** sentences using the words in the box.

   ledge   dodge   wedge   hedgehog   nudge

   a. _____

   b. _____

Suffixes –ed, –ing, –er, –est, –y

Remember

A suffix is any letters added to the end of a word. Remember the following rules when adding –ed, –ing, –er, –est and –y.

Double the last letter of a word if it has a single vowel or consonant before it. For example: 'sto**p**' becomes 'sto**pp**ing'.

Delete the 'e' if it has a consonant before it. For example: 'hi**ke**' becomes 'hi**king**'. The word 'being' does not follow this rule.

Practise

1 Tick to show where the last letter would be doubled when the suffix is added.

flat ☐   jump ☐   swing ☐   clap ☐

2 Sort these words into the table depending on their suffix.

widest   taped   later   baking   tamed   finest   finer

–ed	–ing	–er	–est

Extend

3 Complete these suffix 'sums' by adding the suffix to the word correctly.

a. rob + ed = _____

b. hop + ed = _____

c. tap + ing = _____

d. sun + y = _____

4. Add the suffix –ed, –ing, –er or –est to the word in brackets and complete the sentences.

a. Some people say that owls are the _____ (wise) birds.

b. My best friend is the _____ (nice) person in the whole world.

c. Our cat is _____ (cute) than yours.

d. My dad said we were _____ (be) too noisy in the garden.

Apply

5. Choose a suffix to add to each of the words and write a sentence using the new word. One has been done for you.

| ed | ing | er | est | y |

a. shop *I went shopping with my mum.*

b. drip _____

c. hum _____

d. hot _____

e. fun _____

6. Add one of the suffixes from the box to each of these words, then find the new words in the word search. Use one of the suffixes twice.

R	D	W	S	L	B	P	K	Z	Q
U	S	X	K	P	L	Z	F	N	X
D	J	U	A	W	J	P	W	I	D
E	O	Z	T	I	H	G	X	R	F
S	H	Z	I	D	L	M	R	J	E
T	T	M	N	E	Y	C	D	S	X
H	U	H	G	R	Z	Y	M	G	L
K	X	O	R	I	P	E	S	T	R
U	V	K	O	B	E	C	I	V	C
V	B	I	K	E	D	T	U	Z	T

| ed | est | er | ing |

a. bike _____

b. skate _____

c. wide _____

d. rude _____

e. ripe _____

Suffixes –ment, –ness, –ful, –less, –ly

Remember

If a suffix starts with a consonant, such as –ment or –ness, it is usually added to a word without changing the last letter of the word. For example: 'enjoy' becomes 'enjoyment'.

If the word ends with 'y' and has a consonant before it, change the 'y' to 'i'. For example: 'merry' becomes 'merriment'.

Practise

1 Underline the suffix in each of these words.

   a. homeless

   b. weakness

   c. eventful

   d. amusement

Tip Read from the beginning of the word. See if you can find the whole word that makes sense on its own. The rest of the word that has been added on the end is the suffix.

2 Write the words next to the correct suffix.

> happiness   movement   illness   lifeless   playful
> loveless   punishment   smoothly   powerful   suddenly

   a. –ment _____

   b. –ness _____

   c. –ful _____

   d. –less _____

   e. –ly _____

3 Draw lines to match each word to the correct suffix.

amaze	ful
youth	ly
dead	ment
still	ness

4 Add the suffix –ment, –ness, –full, –less or –ly to the word in brackets and complete the sentences.

a. The dentist _____ (appoint) was at four o'clock.

b. The children _____ (happy) licked their ice creams.

c. Mum said that she had a _____ (weak) for chocolate.

d. The man was _____ (penny).

Apply

5 Write **two** new words for each word by adding either –ness, –ful, –less or –ly. One has been done for you.

hope	weak	plain	mercy
hopeless	_____	_____	_____
hopeful	_____	_____	_____

6 Explain how adding the suffix –ful changes the meaning of the word 'hope'.

_____

_____

Homophones and exception words

Homophones are words that sound the same but have different spellings and meanings. For example: 'A **pair**' means 'two' whereas 'a **pear**' is a type of fruit. Some words do not follow any specific spelling patterns or rules. These are common exception words. A useful way to remember how to spell a common exception word is to use a sentence to remember the letters, called a mnemonic.

Practise

(1) Unscramble the letters to write the word that goes with the picture.

a.

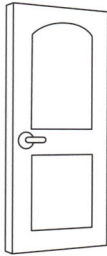

rodo   _____

b.

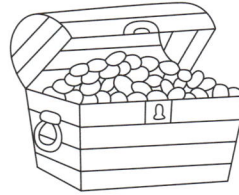

ldgo   _____

c.

rgssa   _____

d.

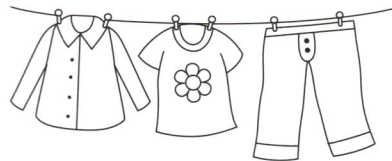

lctohes   _____

Extend

(2) Underline the correct homophone in each sentence.

a. **Hear / Here** is my favourite spot to eat a picnic.

b. The weather is so lovely today, I would rather **be / bee** outside.

c. Ollie had a tasty **stake / steak** for dinner.

d. Mia's hat was **blew / blue** and grey.

③ Write the common exception words from the box in the correct places.

Christmas	pretty	children	fast	plant	cold	people
water	money	idea	Mr	old	improve	busy

_____ Honey found some _____ seeds in the classroom. He told his class they could each grow a _____. They were slow to grow at first, then the _____ gave them some _____. They began to _____. They grew so _____! Before long, the leaves had gone wild, and the flowers were _____ and colourful. One child had a great _____. They would sell the flowers to parents after the _____ concert. Although it was _____, lots of _____ attended and it was _____. The school raised lots of _____ for new books.

Apply

④ Choose **three** pairs of homophones and write a sentence including both homophones. One has been done for you.

a. Homophone pair: _which and witch_

Sentence: _Which witch won the broomstick flying competition?_

b. Homophone pair: _____

Sentence: _____

c. Homophone pair: _____

Sentence: _____

Word choice

Practise

1. Draw lines to match the words that are closest in meaning.

hurry	mouldy
prepare	impressive
rotten	arrange
dangerous	rush
brilliant	risky

2. Circle the odd one out in each set of words.

   a. pretty   dull   beautiful   attractive

   b. shout   look   peep   stare

   c. immense   huge   vast   tiny

   d. pierce   jab   problem   puncture

   e. laugh   sob   weep   cry

Tip   Read all four words. Think about which word has the opposite meaning to the other three words.

Extend

3 Replace the underlined word in each sentence with a word from the box.

a. I was so <u>happy</u> when I heard the news.

_____

difficult   delighted

b. The <u>smell</u> of the rubbish bin was overpowering.

_____

stench   slither

c. My baby sister is so <u>small</u>.

_____

neat   tiny

d. In the book, the <u>evil</u> villain is terrifying.

_____

vile   flat

Apply

4 Rewrite each sentence and choose words to add more detail. One has been done for you.

a. The cat sat on the mat.

<u>The fluffy, white cat snuggled up on the ancient rug.</u>

b. The magician did a trick.

_____

c. Hassan was tired.

_____

5 Write a short description of a place that you love to visit. Think carefully about the words you choose to describe it.

_____

_____

_____

Story language

There are words and phrases that are often used in stories. Using a wide range of vocabulary in stories makes them fun to read and adds detail about characters and settings. Stories often have a clear beginning, middle and end.

Practise

(1) Draw a picture in each box to show what happens in the beginning, middle and end of the story.

> In a land far, far away, a colossal, scaly dragon lived in a cave. He was extremely sad and lonely because he didn't have any friends. One morning, he heard a rumble of thunder and saw a bright flash of light in the sky above. Suddenly, another dragon appeared! Her scales shimmered like jewels in the early morning sunlight. They instantly became friends and the dragon was never lonely again.

Beginning	Middle	End

(2) Write what happens in the story in your own words.

_____

_____

_____

_____

⟫ Extend

3 Write **four** words under each picture to describe the setting or character.

a.

b.

c.

_____   _____   _____

_____   _____   _____

_____   _____   _____

_____   _____   _____

☁ Apply

4 Rewrite this story to make it more interesting by adding more detail and varied vocabulary.

> Once upon a time there was a prince who lived in a castle in a forest. One day, a witch cast a spell on the prince, which turned him into a frog. A princess broke the spell and the frog turned back into a prince. They lived happily ever after.

_____

_____

_____

_____

_____

_____

_____

Topic words

Practise

(1) Choose the correct topic title from the box for each list of words.

> Plants   Dinosaurs   Australia

a.	b.	c.
claw	climate	stem
predator	coral reef	root
scavenger	continent	pollinate
herbivore	population	habitat

Extend

(2) Write labels for the picture. One has been done for you.

arrow slit

3. Circle the odd one out in each set of words.

   a. gills   fin   feet   scales

   b. sail   cockpit   engine   wing

   c. steering wheel   bonnet   boot   paws

Apply

4. Complete these sentences using the words in the box.

> village   prey   city   carnivores
>
> skyscrapers   predators   population

   a. Lions are _____ because they eat other animals. Lions are _____ and chase their _____ when they hunt.

   b. A _____ is bigger than a _____, which can be very small. It has tall, modern buildings called _____. It has a larger _____ too, which means that more people live there.

5. Use the words in **Question 4** to write **four** sentences of your own. One has been done for you.

   a. <u>New York has lots of skyscrapers because it is a large city</u> <u>in America.</u>

   b. _____

   _____

   c. _____

   _____

   d. _____

   _____

Pattan's Pumpkin, by Chitra Soundar

Pattan's Pumpkin is a re-telling of an old Indian story about a man called Pattan. One day, there is a flood. Pattan must work out how to save his family and all the animals.

Once upon a time, there was a man called Pattan. He lived with his wife, Kanni, on the banks of a mighty river that galloped down the Sahyadri mountains.

They tended the goats, fed the bulls and rode with the elephants that roamed their lands.

Pattan grew pepper, rice, nutmeg and bananas. He shared his food with everyone – the animals, the birds and the insects.

One day, Pattan found an ailing plant in the valley. It had beautiful yellow flowers.

"I'll plant it by my hut and look after it," he thought.

The plant liked its new home. Its yellow flowers smiled at the sun.

"Look!" Pattan called one day. "A pumpkin has started to grow."

The pumpkin grew a little every day.

"The goats can't reach it now," said Kanni.

The pumpkin had grown taller than the fence. It was fatter than the pigs. It grew some more. Pattan had to climb on the elephants to check the pumpkin. And still it grew bigger ... and bigger ... and BIGGER.

"Soon it will be as tall as the mountain," said Pattan.

The next day, dark clouds gathered. Rain crashed against the rocks in fury. Pattan was afraid that the floods would wash away his hut.

"We should leave the mountains tomorrow," he said. "We should take all the animals, birds, beetles and bugs with us. And a sapling of every plant and seeds of every grain."

But how were they going to take all the creatures with them?

Pattan couldn't sleep that night. When the pumpkin glowed like fire under a burst of lightning, he had an idea ...

Pattan's Pumpkin, by Chitra Soundar

1 Find and copy **one** word that shows the river was strong.

_____

2 Where did Pattan want to plant the yellow flowers? Tick **one**.

on the banks of the river ☐   by his hut ☐

in the valley ☐   next to the goat pen ☐

3 Tick to show whether each sentence is true or false.

Sentence	True	False
The pumpkin grew all in one day.		
The pumpkin was taller than the fence.		
The pumpkin was fatter than the pigs.		

4 Why was Pattan afraid?

_____

5 *When the pumpkin glowed like a fire under a burst of lightning, he had an idea ...*

What idea do you think Pattan had?

_____

_____

Spelling in Action

And still it grew bigger ... and bigger ... and BIGGER.

The suffix –er shows how big the pumpkin grew. Find and copy **one** other word that uses the –er suffix (see page 40 for the suffix –er).

_____

River Stories, by Timothy Knapman

River Stories is a picture book that takes the reader on a journey along five of the world's rivers. This section is about the Amazon, a large river in South America. It gives facts about the river and also tells stories about its history and mythology.

The Amazon

Flowing from a tangle of rivers in Peru, the Amazon is surrounded by life in all its wonder. One third of all animal and plant species live in its rainforest. The vegetation on its banks is so thick that not a single bridge has been built across it.

Let's paddle down the river and hear its stories. There is magic in these murky waters and, sometimes, danger …

Hidden Villages

In remote areas, deforestation has revealed strange circles – ditches surrounding old settlements from the 15th century. The circles prove that people lived all over the forest, by smaller streams, and not just next to the Amazon River.

Kayak Adventure

In 2010, television presenter Helen Skelton completed the longest solo journey in a kayak, travelling 3235km down the Amazon. Paddling for 12 hours a day for six weeks, she beat foot sores, dehydration, sickness and even the sinking of the kayak!

Dolphin Magic

Strange stories are told about the river's pink dolphins. Some say that if you take a swim alone, they will whisk you off to an underwater city called Encante and you will never return.

The Lost City

In 1930, car maker Henry Ford set up a new town to produce rubber for tyres. The local workers weren't happy at Fordlandia – football was banned and they had to eat unfamiliar food like hamburgers. They revolted, chasing managers onto boats and the cook into the jungle! Later the rubber crop failed and the town was abandoned.

River Stories, by Timothy Knapman

1. Why has a bridge never been built across the Amazon?

_____

2. *There is magic in these murky waters and, sometimes, danger ...*

   Give the heading of the section about the magic in the water.

   _____

3. Look at the section **Hidden Villages**. What have the strange circles proved? Tick **one**.

   Aliens landed there in spaceships. ☐

   People lived all over the forest. ☐

   Animals ate all the grass there. ☐

4. Name **two** difficulties that Helen Skelton beat when she kayaked down the Amazon.

   _____ and _____

5. Complete the table using information from the text.

Time in history	Event
15th century	People lived in villages around and near the Amazon.
	Henry Ford set up a new town.
2010	

Punctuation in Action

*The local workers **weren't** happy at Fordlandia ...*

Which **two** words is 'weren't' short for (see page 26 for apostrophes in shortened forms)?

_____

Mermaid School, by Clare Bevan

'Mermaid School' by Clare Bevan is a modern poem. In it, the poet imagines that mermaids go to school and lists all the skills they could learn there.

What do mermaids learn at school?

How to sing beside a pool.
How to catch a flying fish,
How to grant an Earth-child's wish.
How to chime a ship's old bell,
How to curl inside a shell.
How to win a sea-horse race,
How to swoop and dive and chase.
Faster than the dolphin teams.
How to swim the silver beams
Of the small and misty moon.
How to play a magic tune.
How to tame a hungry shark.
How to find (when nights grow dark)
Hidden caves where treasures lie.
How to read a cloudy sky.
How to make a pearly ring.
How to mend a seabird's wing.
How to use a golden comb.
How to balance on the foam.
How to greet a friendly whale.
How to spin upon your tail.
How to twist and leap and turn ...

This is what the mermaids learn.

Mermaid School, by Clare Bevan

1 List **two** things that a mermaid learns at school.

a. _____

b. _____

2 Which of these words make a rhyming pair? Circle **one**.

pool and fish   chime and curl   bell and shell

3 Why do you think a mermaid might need to 'tame a hungry shark'?

_____

4 Which of these words means the same as 'fix'? Tick **one**.

make ☐   mend ☐   use ☐   spin ☐

5 Which of these skills do you think is the most important for a mermaid to learn? Tick **one**.

to read a cloudy sky ☐   to twist and leap and turn ☐

Explain your answer.

_____

_____

Grammar in Action

Underline the **four** adjectives in these lines of the poem (see page 6 for adjectives).

How to swim the silver beams

Of the small and misty moon.

How to play a magic tune.

Flat Stanley, by Jeff Brown

Flat Stanley follows the adventures of Stanley Lambchop after he is flattened by a bulletin board while sleeping. He soon discovers that there are many advantages to being flat, but it is not always easy being different.

Breakfast was ready.

"I will go wake the boys," Mrs Lambchop said to her husband, George Lambchop. Just then their younger son, Arthur, called from the bedroom he shared with his brother, Stanley.

"Hey! Come and look! Hey!"

Mr and Mrs Lambchop were both very much in favour of politeness and careful speech. "Hay is for horses, Arthur, not people," Mr Lambchop said as they entered the bedroom. "Try to remember that."

"Excuse me," Arthur said. "But look!"

He pointed to Stanley's bed. Across it lay the enormous bulletin board that Mr Lambchop had given the boys a Christmas ago so that they could pin up pictures and messages and maps. It had fallen, during the night, on top of Stanley.

But Stanley was not hurt. In fact he would still have been sleeping if he had not been woken by his brother's shout.

"What's going on here?" he called out cheerfully from beneath the enormous board.

Mr and Mrs Lambchop hurried to lift it from the bed.

"Heavens!" said Mrs Lambchop.

"Gosh!" said Arthur. "Stanley's flat!"

"As a pancake," said Mr Lambchop. "Darndest thing I've ever seen."

"Let's all have breakfast," Mrs Lambchop said. "Then Stanley and I will go see Doctor Dan and hear what he has to say."

In his office, Doctor Dan examined Stanley all over.

The examination was almost over.

"How do you feel?" Doctor Dan asked. "Does it hurt very much?"

"I felt sort of tickly for a while after I got up," Stanley Lambchop said, "but I feel fine now."

"Well, that's mostly how it is with these cases," said Doctor Dan.

"We'll just have to keep an eye on this young fellow," he said when he had finished the examination. "Sometimes we doctors, despite all our years of training and experience, can only marvel at how little we really know."

Mrs Lambchop said she thought that Stanley's clothes would have to be altered by the tailor now, so Doctor Dan told his nurse to take Stanley's measurements.

Mrs Lambchop wrote them down.

Stanley was four feet tall, about a foot wide, and half an inch thick.

When Stanley got used to being flat, he enjoyed it.

He could go in and out of rooms, even when the door was closed, just by lying down and sliding through the crack at the bottom.

Mr and Mrs Lambchop said it was silly, but they were quite proud of him.

Arthur got jealous and tried to slide under a door, but he just banged his head.

Being flat could also be helpful, Stanley found.

He was taking a walk with Mrs Lambchop one afternoon when her favourite ring fell from her finger. The ring rolled across the pavement and down between the bars of a grating that covered a dark, deep shaft.

Mrs Lambchop began to cry.

"I have an idea," Stanley said.

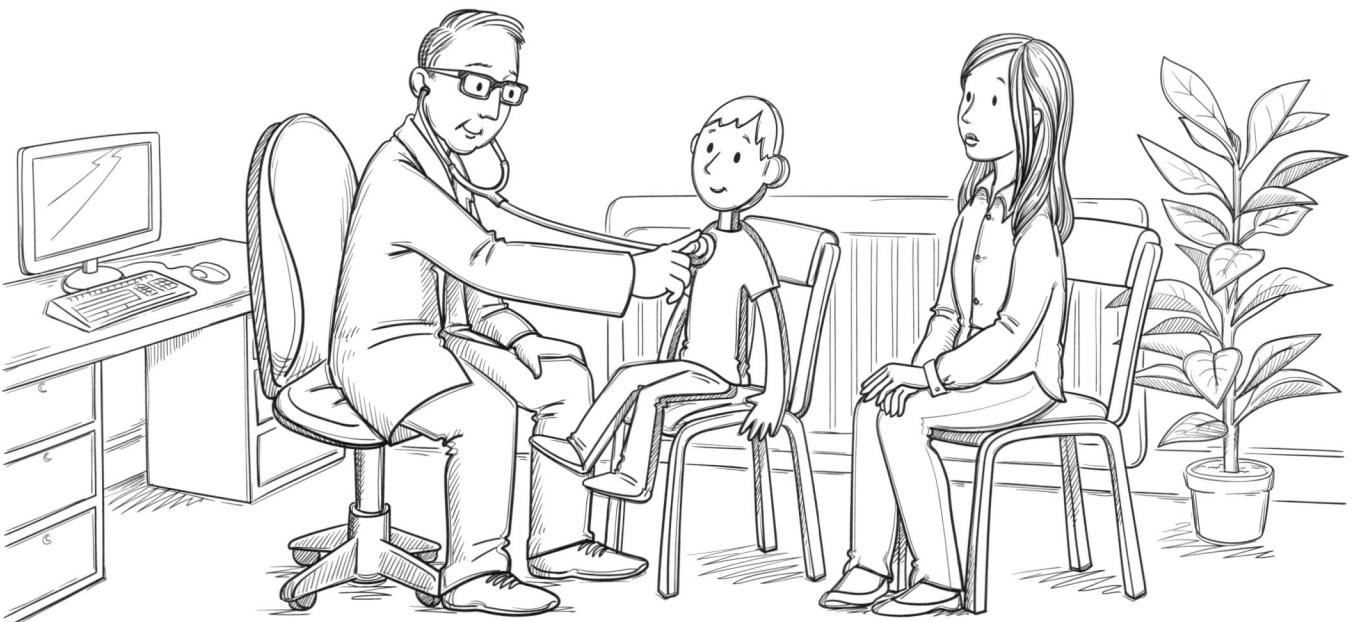

1 **a.** Read from the beginning of the text to ... *Come and look! Hey!"*. What time of day is it? Circle **one**.

evening   morning   afternoon   lunchtime

b. Find and copy **one** word or group of words that supports your answer.

_____

2 *"Hay is for horses, Arthur, not people", Mr Lambchop said as they entered the bedroom.*

Explain how the author has used humour here.

_____

_____

_____

3 Write **two** uses of the bulletin board.

a. _____

b. _____

4 Why did Stanley wake up? Tick **one**.

His brother shouted. ☐

The alarm clock went off. ☐

The board fell on him. ☐

His parents shouted at him. ☐

5 Look at the paragraph beginning *"What's going on here ..."*. Find and copy **one** word from this paragraph that is closest in meaning to the word 'happily'.

_____

6 What does Mr Lambchop compare Stanley to after he becomes flat?

_____

7 How did Stanley feel when he became flat. Tick **one**.

He was in a lot of pain. ☐

He felt tickly but fine. ☐

He felt exactly the same. ☐

He was very upset. ☐

8 Explain the **two** things Stanley does to go in and out of rooms when he is flat.

a. _____

b. _____

9 How did Mrs Lambchop feel when her ring fell from her finger? Explain your answer.

_____

10 _"I have an idea," Stanley said._

What do you think Stanley's idea is?

_____

_____

_____

Vocabulary in Action

"I have an idea," Stanley said.

What word could the author use instead of 'said' (see page 46 for word choice)?

_____

The Bee Book, by Charlotte Milner

> This text is from a book about bees. It gives information about queen bees and about the other types of bee found in hives. The text also answers questions about how bees talk to each other and why they sometimes move in a swarm.

What does the queen do?

A queen is born

When a new queen is needed, the old queen lays an egg in a big cell called a queen cup. A queen egg needs more room to grow than the other eggs, and she needs to eat plenty of royal jelly.

The fight to be queen

There can only be one queen in a nest, so if more than one queen is born, they fight by stinging each other. The survivor is crowned the queen.

Meeting a drone

The queen takes a mating flight to meet a drone bee. She flies to where thousands of drone bees have gathered to meet her. When she returns to the nest she is ready to start laying eggs.

Egg laying

The queen spends her life laying eggs. She can lay as many as one egg every twenty seconds! If she slows down at laying eggs then the colony might replace her with a new queen.

How do honey bees talk to each other?

Honey bees need to be able to tell each other where to find the best flowers. But honey bees can't talk. Instead, they dance! Bees communicate inside the hive using the waggle dance.

When a honey bee does the waggle dance, she walks around in two loops and shakes her body. The angle of the dance tells the other bees the direction of the flowers.

The dance also tells other bees how far away the flowers are. The longer a bee dances for, the further away the flowers are from the hive. A short waggle dance means that the flowers are close.

Honey bees carefully watch the waggle dancer's every move. They even notice the dancer's smell! They smell flowers to find the same type of flower that the dancer visited.

What is a swarm?

A large group of honey bees flying together is called a swarm. A swarm forms when the queen, along with some of the colony, leaves the old nest to find a new nest.

A swarm is made up of one queen and up to 20 000 worker bees. A swarm occurs when a nest becomes overcrowded. Just before a new queen is born into the colony, the old queen gets ready to swarm with around half of the worker bees.

The old queen leaves with the swarm to find a new nest, while the new queen is left behind with the rest of the bees.

The bees prepare for their long flight by eating lots of honey to give them energy. But the queen is not a strong flier, so the swarm may have to stop along the way to let her rest.

Even though a swarm of bees may look scary, they are not usually dangerous. As long as their hunt for a home doesn't get disturbed, then they will not sting.

The Bee Book, by Charlotte Milner

① What is the name of the 'cell' where the queen lays her eggs?

_____

② What does a queen bee eat?

_____

③ Read the section **The fight to be queen**. In your own words, explain what happens if more than one queen is born.

_____

_____

_____

④ What might happen to a queen bee if she slows down at laying eggs?

_____

_____

⑤ Read the section **Meeting a drone**. Number the sentences 1 to 4 to show the order of the events.

The queen is ready to start laying eggs.   ____

The queen returns to the nest.   ____

The queen flies to meet a drone bee.   ____

The queen meets thousands of drone bees.   ____

⑥ Read the section **How do honey bees talk to each other?**. Find and copy **one** word that means the same as 'talk'.

_____

7 Why do honey bees dance? Tick **two**.

to show how much they love music ☐

to tell each other where to find the best flowers ☐

to shake the pollen from their bodies ☐

to tell other bees how far away the flowers are ☐

8 What does it mean if the honey bee does a short 'waggle dance'?

_____

9 Why do bees smell flowers?

_____

_____

10 Tick to show whether each sentence is true or false.

Statement	True	False
A swarm is made up of one queen bee and many worker bees.		
The old queen stays in the nest.		
The queen is not a strong flier.		
Swarms of bees are very angry.		

Spelling in Action

Even though a swarm of bees may look scary, they are not usually dangerous.

Which word in the sentence contains the /or/ sound spelt 'ar' (see page 30 for the /or/ sound spelt 'ar')?

_____

Here are two poems about minibeasts. In the first poem, someone is holding a ladybird. The person in the second poem has a worm. Read both poems to see the similarities and differences between them.

The Ladybird, by Clive Sansom

Tiniest of turtles!
Your shining back
Is a shell of orange
With spots of black.

How trustingly you walk
Across this land
Of hairgrass and hollows
That is my hand.

Your small wire legs,
So frail, so thin,
Their touch is swansdown
Upon my skin.

There! break out
Your wings and fly:
No tenderer creature
Beneath the sky.

The Worm, by Ralph Bergengren

When the earth is turned in spring
The worms are fat as anything.

And birds come flying all around
To eat the worms right off the ground.

They like worms just as much as I
Like bread and milk and apple pie.

And once, when I was very young,
I put a worm right on my tongue.

I didn't like the taste a bit,
And so I didn't swallow it.

But oh, it makes my Mother squirm
Because she *thinks* I ate that worm!

Comparing texts: poems about minibeasts

1 Which **two** colours are the ladybird in the poem 'The Ladybird'?
Tick **one**.

red and black ☐

black and orange ☐

black and white ☐

pink and yellow ☐

2 Why does the poet compare the ladybird to a turtle?

_____

_____

3 Find and copy **one** word that shows the ladybird was comfortable walking across the poet's hand.

_____

4 How does the ladybird feel on the poet's skin? Circle **one**.

hairy and tickly   wet and cold

light and soft   rough and prickly

5 Do you think the poet likes ladybirds? Tick **one**.

Yes ☐   No ☐

Explain your answer using an example from the text.

_____

_____

_____

(6) Which **three** foods and drinks does the poet of 'The Worm' like?

a. _____

b. _____

c. _____

(7) Why did the poet not swallow the worm?

_____

(8) Why do you think the poet has chosen the verb 'squirm' to describe what his mother does?

_____

_____

(9) Name **one** thing that both the poems have in common.

_____

_____

(10) Which poem do you like best? Tick **one**.

'The Ladybird' ☐   'The Worm' ☐

Explain your answer.

_____

_____

_____

Grammar in Action

Which adjective does the poet use to describe the worms in spring (see page 6 for adjectives)?

_____

The Velveteen Rabbit, by Margery Williams

This text is part of a story about a toy rabbit. The toy rabbit is made of a material called velveteen and it lives in a boy's bedroom. It wants to know the difference between being a toy and being real.

"What is REAL?" asked the Rabbit one day, when they were lying side by side near the nursery fender, before Nana came to tidy the room. "Does it mean having things that buzz inside you and a stick-out handle?"

"Real isn't how you are made," said the Skin Horse. "It's a thing that happens to you. When a child loves you for a long, long time, not just to play with, but REALLY loves you, then you become Real."

"Does it hurt?" asked the Rabbit.

"Sometimes," said the Skin Horse, for he was always truthful. "When you are Real you don't mind being hurt."

"Does it happen all at once, like being wound up," he asked, "or bit by bit?"

"It doesn't happen all at once," said the Skin Horse. "You become. It takes a long time. That's why it doesn't often happen to people who break easily, or have sharp edges, or who have to be carefully kept. Generally, by the time you are Real, most of your hair has been loved off, and your eyes drop out and you get loose in the joints and very shabby. But these things don't matter at all, because once you are Real you can't be ugly, except to people who don't understand."

"I suppose *you* are real?" said the Rabbit. And then he wished he had not said it, for he thought the Skin Horse might be sensitive. But the Skin Horse only smiled.

"The Boy's Uncle made me Real," he said. "That was a great many years ago; but once you are Real you can't become unreal again."

The Rabbit sighed. He thought it would be a long time before this magic called Real happened to him. He longed to become Real, to know what it felt like; and yet the idea of growing shabby and losing his eyes and whiskers was rather sad. He wished that he could become it without these uncomfortable things happening to him.

There was a person called Nana who ruled the nursery. Sometimes she took no notice of the playthings lying about, and sometimes, for no reason whatever, she went swooping about like a great wind and hustled them away in cupboards. She called this 'tidying up,' and the playthings all hated it, especially the tin ones. The Rabbit didn't mind it so much, for whenever he was thrown he came down soft.

One evening, when the Boy was going to bed, he couldn't find the china dog that always slept with him. Nana was in a hurry, and it was too much trouble to hunt for china dogs at bedtime, so she simply looked about her, and seeing that the toy cupboard door stood open, she made a swoop.

"Here," she said, "take your old Bunny! He'll do to sleep with you!" And she dragged the Rabbit out by one ear, and put him into the Boy's arms.

That night, and for many nights after, the Velveteen Rabbit slept in the Boy's bed. At first he found it rather uncomfortable, for the Boy hugged him very tight, and sometimes he rolled over on him, and sometimes he pushed him so far under the pillow that the Rabbit could scarcely breathe. And he missed, too, those long moonlight hours in the nursery, when all the house was silent, and his talks with the Skin Horse. But very soon he grew to like it, for the Boy used to talk to him, and made nice tunnels for him under the bedclothes that he said were like the burrows the real rabbits lived in.

The Velveteen Rabbit, by Margery Williams

(1) What type of room are the Rabbit and the Skin Horse in? Tick **one**.

a nursery ☐   a classroom ☐

a dining room ☐   a kitchen ☐

(2) *"When a child loves you for a really long, long time, not just to play with, but REALLY loves you, then you become Real."*

Why do you think the word 'really' is written in capital letters?

_____

(3) Tick to show whether each sentence is true or false.

Statement	True	False
It sometimes hurts to become Real.		
Becoming Real happens immediately.		
Once you are Real, you cannot become unreal again.		

(4) *He longed to become Real, to know what it felt like; and yet the idea of growing shabby and losing his eyes and whiskers was rather sad.*

Find and copy **one** word from this sentence that means the same as 'scruffy'.

_____

(5) *... she went swooping about like a great wind and hustled them away in cupboards.*

What does this description tell you about how Nana moved? Circle **one**.

She was slow.   She was gentle.

She was quick.   She was horrible.

(6) Look at the paragraph beginning *There was a person called Nana ...* What did the playthings hate Nana doing?

_____

(7) Why do you think the tin playthings really hated being thrown in the cupboards?

_____

_____

(8) Why did Nana give the Rabbit to the boy?

_____

_____

(9) Do you think the Rabbit liked sleeping in the Boy's bed? Tick **one**.

Yes ☐   No ☐   Sometimes ☐

Explain your answer.

_____

_____

_____

(10) Do you think the Rabbit will ever become 'Real'? Tick **one**.

Yes ☐   No ☐

Explain your answer.

_____

_____

Punctuation in Action

"Does it mean having things that buzz inside you and a stick-out handle?"

The author uses '?' at the end of this sentence (see page 24 for using different punctuation). Why?

_____

Amazing Animals, by Emma Scott

> This non-fiction text gives its readers information about some animals. These animals are all strange or unusual in some way. Read on to find out some interesting facts.

From tiny ants to gigantic whales, there are millions of animals living here on planet Earth. Animals can be found in lots of different habitats around the world. They come in all shapes, sizes and colours and are all unique in their own special ways. But some animals are more unusual than others!

Hummingbirds

Hummingbirds are small nectar-feeding birds named for the humming sound created by their fast, beating wings. Some hummingbirds can flap their wings up to 200 times a second. Their constant wing flapping takes up so much of their energy that they need to eat up to eight times their body weight in food every day.

These beautiful, jewel-coloured birds can be found all over the Americas. Their little feet are so tiny that they can't walk on the ground. However, they can hover and they can fly in many different directions. Did you know that they can fly forwards, backwards and even upside down?

Komodo Dragons

Komodo dragons are one of the largest reptiles on Earth and also one of the deadliest. They were discovered in 1912, when a group of pearl fishermen working in the treacherous waters of Indonesia spotted gigantic lizards patrolling the beach.

With their large bodies, strong necks and powerful limbs, Komodo dragons are fierce carnivores and will eat almost anything they can catch. They have even been known to hunt humans, although these attacks are rare. They have very smelly breath due to the deadly bacteria that can be found in their mouths.

Platypuses

Platypuses are very odd animals that can only be found in Australia. Why exactly are they so strange? Although they are mammals, they also have body parts that normally belong to birds and amphibians. They have furry bodies, beaks and webbed feet. They look so odd that when one was first discovered, scientists thought it was a fake animal, made from lots of pieces sewn together!

Another thing that makes platypuses so unusual is that they don't do some of the things mammals normally do. Usually, mammals give birth to live babies, but female platypuses lay eggs. The platypus is also one of the few mammals that produces venom. Male platypuses store venom in their hind legs and even have a spur, which is a bit like a stinger, on their heel. They use their spur to inject the venom.

Hammerhead Sharks

A hammerhead shark looks very strange indeed. It has a wide, flattened head, in the shape of a hammer, with an eye on each side of it. Their heads move from side to side when they swim and sensors on their head help them to find food. When they find a stingray (their favourite food), they use their unique head as a weapon, pinning it down before eating it.

Hammerhead sharks can be found worldwide in warm, tropical waters. They usually swim in schools (groups) during the day, but they prefer to hunt alone at night.

Mantises

Mantises may be small, but they are deadly hunters in the insect world. They are extremely good at camouflage, often taking on the exact appearance of a flower or leaf. A mantis will find a good hiding spot and wait perfectly still until a tasty morsel gets close enough for it to make its move.

Mantises have huge eyes which help them to spot their prey. They grab their meal with their spiky front legs. Then, they use their strong, powerful jaws to eat their food. Their menu can consist of insects, spiders, mice, frogs or even lizards.

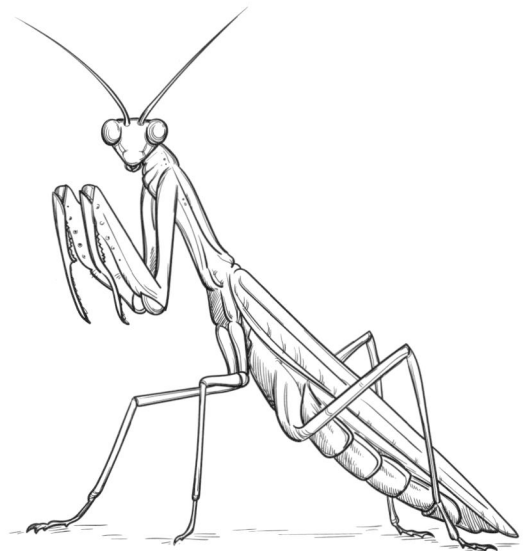

Amazing Animals, by Emma Scott

1 What do hummingbirds' tiny feet stop them from doing?

_____

2 *These beautiful, jewel-coloured birds ...*

Why do you think the author has used these words to describe the hummingbirds?

_____

_____

3 Describe **two** features of Komodo dragons that make them fierce.

a. _____

b. _____

4 Why do Komodo dragons have smelly breath?

_____

5 What type of animal is a platypus? Circle **one**.

fish   bird   amphibian   mammal

6 How do hammerhead sharks find their food?

_____

_____

7 How do mantises camouflage themselves?

_____

_____

(8) Write the numbers 1 to 5 to show the order in which mantises find and eat their food. One has been done for you.

They use their huge eyes to spot their prey. ____

They wait perfectly still. ____

They use their jaws to eat their food. ____

They find a good hiding spot. _1_

They grab their meal with spiky front legs. ____

(9) Write **one** food that each animal eats.

(**Hummingbird**)   (**Hammerhead shark**)   (**Mantis**)

_____   _____   _____

(10) Complete the table to show where each animal lives.

Animal	Where in the world it lives
hummingbird	
Komodo dragon	Indonesia
	worldwide
platypus	

Vocabulary in Action

They were discovered in 1912, when a group of pearl fishermen working in the treacherous waters of Indonesia spotted gigantic lizards patrolling the beach.

Circle the word that is closest in meaning to 'treacherous' (see page 46 for word choice).

calm   dangerous   blue   dirty

Coming Out of Hibernation, by Pie Corbett

'Coming Out of Hibernation' is a poem that looks at the differences between winter and spring. It describes how animals behave when they are in hibernation and then what happens when they wake up.

Black bats hang in barns,
Their wings folded
Like old umbrellas.

Snoring hedgehogs sleep
Curled up tight,
Like hairbrushes
Beneath crisp leaves.

Grey squirrels dream in dreys
Of scrambled twigs.

Toads squat,
Their eyelids drawn down.
As still as stones
Tucked beneath
The compost heap.

Sly spring sunlight
Creeps through clouds;
Bulbs break the warm earth
And the world wears
A new coat.

Bats unfurl their creased wings
And blink their way
From hollow tree stumps.

Hedgehogs uncurl
And sniff, sipping the sunlight.

The blotched toad
Gulps in warm air –
He puffs his wrinkled cheeks
Like an old man.

The squirrel arches her back
And tests a branch;
Before running
Like a rat
To find her acorn stash.

The world rolls onto its side
And stretches out its legs.
Reaching for its sunglasses,
It rubs its earthy hands.

The spring sings out loud.

Coming Out of Hibernation, by Pie Corbett

(1) What does the poet compare the bats' wings to?

_____

(2) Why do you think the poet describes the hedgehogs as being 'like hairbrushes'?

_____

_____

(3) What is the squirrel's 'drey' made from?

_____

(4) Draw lines to match each of the animals to a place they can be found in the poem. One has been done for you.

bats	beneath the compost heap
hedgehogs	in barns
squirrels	beneath leaves
toads	in dreys

(5) Look at the fifth verse. Find and copy **one** word that means the same as 'sneaky'.

_____

(6) Which change of season is being described in the poem? Tick **one**.

summer to autumn ☐   autumn to winter ☐

winter to spring ☐   spring to summer ☐

7 Find and copy **one** group of words that shows why the toad is compared to an old man.

_____

8 What does the squirrel do before finding her acorn stash? Circle **all** the correct answers.

She arches her back.   She swings on a branch.

She meets a rat.   She tests a branch.

9 Number the statements to show the order that the world does things in the poem. One has been done for you.

It reaches for its sunglasses.   ____

It rubs its earthy hands.   ____

It wears a new coat.   _1_

It rolls onto its side.   ____

It stretches out its legs   ____

10 Tick **one** animal. Explain how it changes from the beginning of the poem to the end of the poem.

bat ☐   hedgehog ☐   squirrel ☐   toad ☐

_____

_____

_____

Grammar in Action

Find and copy **two** verbs the poet uses to describe what the hedgehogs are doing (see page 12 for verbs).

_____ and _____

Writing skills: Zookeeper for a Day

The Writing skills task is inspired by the themes in the reading comprehension texts. It provides an opportunity to apply the skills practised in this book. Answer guidance can be downloaded from the **Schofield & Sims** website.

Imagine that you are a zookeeper for the day. You must look after everything from elephants to penguins. Write an account of a day in your life as a zookeeper, describing what you do, which animals you take care of and how you look after them. Think about what the animals look like, how they move, what they need and how you are feeling. Use the prompt sentence below to begin your account if you wish to.

You could use some of the following in your account:

- adjectives (page 6)
- expanded noun phrases (page 8)
- verbs (page 12)
- joining words (page 18)
- story language (page 48).

Re-read 'Amazing Animals' (page 74) for some ideas.

I pulled on my boots and got a big bucket of food ready.

_____

_____

_____

_____

_____

_____

_____

Final practice

The Final practice includes grammar, punctuation, spelling, vocabulary and reading comprehension questions. Work through the questions carefully and try to answer each one. The target time for completing these questions is 45 minutes. The answers can be downloaded from the **Schofield & Sims** website.

1 Tick to show which word class the words in the table belong to.

Word	Noun	Adjective	Verb
a. Saturday			
b. skipped			
c. gentle			

1 mark

2 a. Underline the verb in this sentence.

The man ran to the bus stop.

b. Rewrite the sentence using an adverb to describe the verb.

_____

1 mark

3 Rewrite the sentence in the past tense.

I am having a fantastic time on holiday.

_____

1 mark

4 Read the sentences below. Underline the expanded noun phrase in each sentence.

a. Maria chose a hot chocolate in the cosy, warm café.

b. When it got dark, I put bright, shiny reflectors on my bicycle.

1 mark

5 Rewrite the underlined word in each sentence to add an apostrophe.

a. <u>Weve</u> made Dad a cake for his birthday. _____

b. The park was the <u>buss</u> final stop. _____

1 mark

6 Write **one** sentence of each type about the picture.

   a. Statement:

   _____

   b. Question:

   _____

1 mark

7 Write a sentence using these words and some commas to make a list of the things needed to bake a cake.

| butter   flour   sugar   three eggs   jam   strawberries |

Yan is going to make a cake with _____

_____

1 mark

8 Rewrite this sentence using the correct punctuation.

on sunday, we are going on holiday to france

_____

1 mark

9 Read the clues and write the missing words.

   a. the pieces of paper that make up a book _____

   b. the place in your leg where it bends _____

   c. what you write and draw with _____

1 mark

10 Complete these suffix 'sums' by adding the suffix to the word correctly.

   a. copy + ed _____

   b. bubble + ing _____

1 mark

11 Tick to show if the word is spelt correctly. If the word has been spelt incorrectly, write the correct spelling on the line.

a. competition ☐ _____

b. babys ☐ _____

1 mark

12 Choose the correct words from the box to complete the sentence.

| bear | bare | two | too | to |

I went _____ the zoo and saw a _____ .

1 mark

13 Circle the words that are spelt incorrectly in this text. Write the correct spellings on the line.

Jack planted seeds and gave them worter. The seeds grew into a beanstalk. Jack climed the beanstalk becos he hoped to find some guld.

_____

1 mark

14 Replace each underlined word with another word that has a similar meaning.

a. The witch was <u>ugly</u>. _____

b. We <u>walked</u> to the park. _____

c. The gingerbread house was <u>yummy</u>. _____

1 mark

15 Tick the **three** words that would be the best words to label this picture.

beak ☐   nice ☐   toes ☐

wing ☐   claws ☐   cute ☐

1 mark

Final practice

The Tale of Peter Rabbit, by Beatrix Potter

> Peter Rabbit is a wild rabbit. One day, he sneaks into Mr McGregor's garden and eats his vegetables. In this text, Mr McGregor has just chased Peter away from his vegetables and Peter is hiding from the gardener in an unpleasant, wet watering can.

Mr McGregor was quite sure that Peter was somewhere in the toolshed, perhaps hidden underneath a flower-pot. He began to turn them over carefully, looking under each.

Presently Peter sneezed – "Kertyshoo!" Mr McGregor was after him in no time.

And tried to put his foot upon Peter, who jumped out of a window, upsetting three plants. The window was too small for Mr McGregor, and he was tired of running after Peter. He went back to his work.

Peter sat down to rest; he was out of breath and trembling with fright, and he had not the least idea which way to go. Also he was very damp with sitting in that can.

After a time he began to wander about, going lippity–lippity–not very fast, and looking all around.

He found a door in a wall; but it was locked, and there was no room for a fat little rabbit to squeeze underneath.

An old mouse was running in and out over the stone doorstep, carrying peas and beans to her family in the wood. Peter asked her the way to the gate, but she had such a large pea in her mouth that she could not answer. She only shook her head at him. Peter began to cry.

Then he tried to find his way straight across the garden, but he became more and more puzzled. Presently, he came to a pond where Mr McGregor filled his water-cans. A white cat was staring at some goldfish; she sat very, very still, but now and then the tip of her tail twitched as if it were alive. Peter thought it best to go away without speaking to her; he had heard about cats from his cousin, little Benjamin Bunny.

16 Why did Mr McGregor turn over the flower-pots?

_____

_____

1 mark

17 Look at the first **two** paragraphs. Find and copy **one** group of words that shows Mr McGregor hurried to catch Peter.

_____

1 mark

18 Tick to show whether each sentence is true or false.

Statement	True	False
Mr McGregor climbed out of the window.		
Peter was lost.		
Peter was comfortable sitting in the can.		
Peter knocked over three plants.		

3 marks

19 Write **two** problems that Peter had when he found a door in the wall.

a. _____

b. _____

2 marks

20 Which **two** things was the old mouse carrying?

_____ and _____

1 mark

21 What do you think Benjamin Bunny might have told Peter about cats? Write what you think he might have said in the speech bubble.

2 marks

Total:

25 marks